C000090199

DOD Personnel: Improvements Made to Housing Allowance Rate-Setting Process: GAO-01-508

U.S. Government Accountability Office (GAO)

The BiblioGov Project is an effort to expand awareness of the public documents and records of the U.S. Government via print publications. In broadening the public understanding of government and its work, an enlightened democracy can grow and prosper. Ranging from historic Congressional Bills to the most recent Budget of the United States Government, the BiblioGov Project spans a wealth of government information. These works are now made available through an environmentally friendly, print-on-demand basis, using only what is necessary to meet the required demands of an interested public. We invite you to learn of the records of the U.S. Government, heightening the knowledge and debate that can lead from such publications.

Included are the following Collections:

Budget of The United States Government
Presidential Documents
United States Code
Education Reports from ERIC
GAO Reports
History of Bills
House Rules and Manual
Public and Private Laws

Code of Federal Regulations
Congressional Documents
Economic Indicators
Federal Register
Government Manuals
House Journal
Privacy act Issuances
Statutes at Large

GAO

April 2001

DOD PERSONNEL

Improvements Made to Housing Allowance Rate-Setting Process

GAO
Accountability ★ Integrity ★ Reliability

GAO-01-508

Contents

United States General Accounting Office
Washington, DC 20548

April 16, 2001

The Honorable John M. McHugh
Chairman
The Honorable Martin T. Meehan
Ranking Minority Member
Subcommittee on Military Personnel
Committee on Armed Services
House of Representatives

The Honorable Mike Thompson
House of Representatives

About two-thirds of the married and one-third of the single
servicemembers in the United States live in private housing in the
communities surrounding military installations. These members are given
a cash housing allowance, called the basic allowance for housing, to help
defray the cost of renting or buying housing. In fiscal year 2000, housing
allowances totaled about $6.0 billion and covered about 81 percent of the
typical member's housing and utility costs, with the member paying the
remaining costs out-of-pocket. The National Defense Authorization Act for
Fiscal Year 1998[1] required the Department of Defense (DOD) to make
changes in the allowance program intended to better match the allowance
rates with the actual costs of local housing in various geographic areas of
the country. DOD began these changes in January 1998 and planned to
implement them over a 6-year period ending in 2003. DOD officials knew
that the changes would cause some rates to rise and others to decline.
However, in January 2000, rate decreases outnumbered the increases and
were substantial in some cases. Compared to 1999 levels, rates declined by
over $200 a month for some servicemembers, and DOD decreased rates in
some areas in which housing costs were rapidly increasing.

In response to your concerns about DOD's housing allowance rate-setting
process and the downward change in many January 2000 rates, we
determined (1) the reasons for the rate decreases, (2) DOD's response to
the concerns about the decreases, and (3) actions that might be taken to
improve the rate-setting process.

---

[1]See Pub. L. 105-85, sec. 603, codified at 37 U.S.C. 403.

GAO-01-508 Military Personnel

Results in Brief

In January 2000, many housing allowance rates declined simply because DOD changed the way it determines housing allowances. Previously, DOD based allowances primarily on servicemembers' expenditures for housing in each geographic area. Under the new program, DOD bases allowances on the local costs for the "housing standard" that DOD sets for each servicemember's rank (e.g. the "housing standard" for a private with dependents is a two-bedroom apartment). This change increased allowances in areas where members had been spending less for housing than the local cost of the housing under DOD's standards. Conversely, the change decreased allowances in areas where members had been spending more for housing than the local costs of the housing under DOD's standards. DOD had planned a phased transition of the new program to moderate rate and budgetary impacts. However, to benefit members living in high-cost areas, the Congress authorized additional funding to allow DOD to accelerate implementation of market-based housing allowance rates.[2] In other geographic areas, the accelerated implementation also resulted in more widespread and dramatic rate decreases.

DOD responded quickly to concerns about the rates and began a review of its rate-setting process in January 2000. DOD determined that although the local housing cost data used to establish the rates was accurate, the rate-setting process included shortcomings which could, and did in at least one geographic area, result in rates being set too low. For example, in the Tacoma, Washington area, DOD concluded that the 2000 housing allowance rates were set too low because some inappropriate rental housing units were included in the samples used to determine local housing costs. In view of its findings, DOD decided in March 2000 to revert to the higher 1999 rates in all areas where rates had decreased. DOD also implemented several changes, including increasing the participation of local installation officials to improve the process used to determine rates for 2001. DOD and service headquarters officials believe that the changes have been successfully implemented and that the January 2001 rates are fair and accurate in all areas of the country.

Further improvements to the rate setting process are possible. First, concerns remain regarding the housing standards DOD uses to determine allowance rates, including whether the standards associated with the military ranks are appropriate and whether the standards should be the same for members living in privately owned and government-owned

---

[2]See the National Defense Authorization Act for Fiscal Year 2000, Pub. L. 106-65, sec. 603.

housing. DOD has initiated a study to look at the issues related to housing standards and allowance rates. Second, DOD could better inform installation officials how the final housing allowance rates for their areas are determined each year, thereby increasing local confidence in the process. Because DOD does not now routinely provide this information, local managers lack assurance that the rates are well-supported and calculated correctly. Further, when members question how their rates were determined, installation officials cannot provide specific details, such as the local housing and utility costs estimates used to determine the rates and DOD's adjustments, if any, to the cost data when determining the final rates.

We are recommending that the Secretary of Defense provide housing officials at each major installation detailed information showing the basis for the annual allowance rates established for the installation. In its comments on our draft report, DOD agreed with the recommendation.

Background

The intent of the basic allowance for housing program is to provide servicemembers with accurate and equitable housing compensation when government housing is not provided. The Under Secretary of Defense for Personnel and Readiness is responsible for administering the basic allowance for housing program. Similar to other DOD compensation programs, the housing allowance program is managed centrally with allowance rates applying equally to servicemembers in all military services.

The legislation establishing the program required that rates be based on the cost of adequate housing for civilians with comparable incomes and that the rates vary by a member's rank or pay grade; dependency status, that is, either with or without dependents; and geographic location.[3] To do this, DOD established six housing standards, ranging from a one-bedroom apartment to a four-bedroom, single-family detached house and applied a standard to each military pay grade. Annually, from May through July, DOD uses a contractor to determine the average costs, including utilities and renter's insurance, to rent adequate housing of each standard type in about 350 geographic areas of the United States. After analyzing this information, making adjustments to the data in some cases and deducting the amount of the housing costs that the typical member is expected to

---

[3]See 37 U.S.C. 403.

pay out-of-pocket, DOD sets the rates that become effective on January 1. The appendix provides further details concerning the six housing standards and the way rates are determined.

Just over half of the local housing allowance rates for members with dependents that became effective on January 1, 2000, decreased from 1999 levels. The decreases caused many servicemembers and installation officials to question the fairness and accuracy of the rate-setting process. DOD officials did not anticipate the level of concern caused by the rate decreases because the program includes a provision called rate protection. Under rate protection, members already living in an area with declining rates continue to receive the old allowance rate. The new lower rates apply only to members that move into the affected areas and assuming that the rates were accurately set, these members should be able to find affordable housing based on the new rates. However, rate protection permits servicemembers in the same pay grade at the same installation to receive different allowances depending on when they moved to the installation. In January 2000, the differences in allowances for similarly-situated servicemembers were significant at some installations, and many members did not view this as fair.

Also, in January 2000, shortly after the lower allowances became effective, the Secretary of Defense announced a major new quality-of-life initiative to increase housing allowances across the board by eliminating the average out-of-pocket costs over the next 5 years. Announcing an initiative to increase housing allowances in the same month that DOD reduced many allowances caused some members to raise additional questions about consistency and fairness in the housing allowance program.

Accelerated Implementation of the New Allowance Program Caused Dramatic Rate Decreases

Although DOD's rate-setting process included some shortcomings that could result in some rates being set lower than warranted, the primary reasons for the rate decreases in January 2000 were the change from an allowance program based on expenditures for housing to a program based on housing standards and the accelerated implementation of the new program 3 years earlier than originally planned.

Responding to the concerns about the 2000 rates, DOD began in January 2000 to review the allowance program and the reasons that many rates declined. DOD concluded that most of the rate decreases effective in January 2000 were not caused by a faulty rate development process, but rather by implementation of the new program and the associated change in the way housing allowances are determined. Under the prior allowance program, DOD established allowances partially on the basis of members' expenditures for housing. DOD conducted an annual member survey to collect actual expenditures for housing and utilities. On the basis of the data collected for each pay grade and in each geographic area, DOD established a variable portion of the housing allowance. The variable portion was added to a fixed amount for each pay grade to determine the total housing allowance for each area of the country.

According to DOD, the previous allowance program created some problems, such as large differences in the average out-of-pocket housing costs incurred by members of the same pay grade who lived in different parts of the country. Also, depending on the kind, size, and quality of housing that members were renting, the previous program could cause allowances to be lower or higher than expected. For example, in high cost areas, members often spent less than normally expected on housing by obtaining smaller and less desirable housing. When reporting their housing expenditures in the annual survey, this could result in keeping allowances lower than would be expected based on the cost of local housing. In other areas, where members chose to obtain larger and more expensive housing, the opposite effect could occur, resulting in higher-than-expected allowances.

The new housing allowance program was intended to address these problems and improve equity by using as the basis for the allowances the local costs of defined housing standards applied to each pay grade. The goal was to set rates so that regardless of the assigned location within the United States, a typical servicemember in a particular pay grade could obtain the same type of housing and pay the same average amount out-of-pocket. Also, by using local housing costs as the basis for allowances instead of member housing expenditures, the new program eliminated the downward and upward allowance biases we noted.

The change to the new allowance program tended to increase allowances in areas where the typical member had been spending less for housing than the average local cost of the housing standard set for the member's rank. Conversely, the change tended to decrease allowances in areas where the typical member had been spending more for housing than the average local cost of the housing standard set for the member's rank. To illustrate, the DOD housing standard for a member with dependents in pay grade E-5 is a two-bedroom townhouse or duplex. However, at a particular installation, most E-5 members with dependents might have been renting three-bedroom townhouses or single family homes and spending more for housing than the average cost of a two-bedroom townhouse in the local community. Under the prior allowance program, the allowance for these members would have been based on their actual expenditures for the larger housing units. Because the allowance for E-5 members under the new program is based on the average local cost of the two-bedroom townhouse, implementation of the program would result in decreased allowances for these members. Although the members could choose to continue to spend more for housing, they would have to spend a greater amount out-of-pocket.

Faster Transition to New Housing Allowance Program

Facing the change to a completely new housing allowance program, DOD anticipated that some difficulties would be experienced as the program was implemented. To help mitigate potential problems, DOD originally planned to phase implementation of the new allowance program over a 6-year transition period, starting in 1998. According to DOD officials, the transition period would allow more time for DOD to perfect the new rate-setting process as experience was gained each year, spread the budgetary impact from the new program over a longer period, and moderate expected increases and decreases in allowance rates resulting from the new program.

During the transition years, in areas where the new rate process indicated allowances should increase, DOD planned to limit the size of the actual increase to the rates calculated under the previous allowance program plus a percentage of the difference between those rates and rates calculated under the new rate process. For 2000, the third year of transition, the planned adjustment was 50 percent of the difference between the old and new rates. Similarly, in areas where the new rate process indicated that allowances should decrease, DOD planned to limit the actual amount of the decrease.

In 1999, the Congress authorized DOD to speed up implementation of market-based basic allowance for housing rates.[4] DOD officials stated that

---

[4]See the National Defense Authorization Act for Fiscal Year 2000, Pub. L. 106-65, sec. 603.

accelerated implementation benefited members living in areas where rates were increasing because the amount of the increases would not be limited by the transition plans. In areas where rates were decreasing, however, full implementation also meant that the amount of the decreases would not be limited. DOD did not believe that members in these areas would be negatively impacted because under the program's rate protection provision, the lower rates would apply only to members moving into the affected areas. When the full transition to the new program was completed in January 2000, allowance rates were fully based on the local cost of the housing standards for the first time, resulting in greater rate increases and decreases than would have occurred under the transition plan.

DOD Responded Quickly to Concerns About the Rates

DOD began its review of the new allowance program in January 2000 shortly after the new rates became effective and members began to question the rates. From the review, DOD concluded that the local housing cost data collected and used to determine the January 2000 rates was accurate, and that the change to the new program was the primary cause for the rate decreases. However, DOD concluded that other aspects of the rate-setting process included shortcomings that could, and did in at least one location, result in rates being set too low. In March 2000, DOD took steps to address these shortcomings and improve the rate-setting process it used to determine the 2001 housing allowance rates.

Contractor Developed Accurate Housing Cost Data

Like DOD, we found that the contractor followed reasonable procedures to ensure that the housing data collected was accurate. To help ensure accuracy, the contractor, a recognized leader in the field of collecting cost-of-living data, used several data verification techniques and had an independent housing expert review and critique its data collection methods.

To compare the contractor's local housing cost data with another source, we performed a limited analysis. For 12 geographic areas representing a cross section of urban and rural areas, we compared the contractor's monthly rental cost estimates with the Department of Housing and Urban Development's (HUD) fair market rent estimates for the same areas. The two estimates are not directly comparable due to differences in methodology and time frames. Nevertheless, we found that on average the contractor's rental cost estimates were 17 percent higher than HUD's estimates. This was expected because the contractor screens out many rental units considered unacceptable for military members. The contractor's estimates were lower than HUD's estimates only for one area, and the average difference in the estimates for this area was $27, or 4 percent. In this case, the contractor's estimates were based on the area immediately surrounding the military installation, which was mostly rural. HUD's estimates, however, were based on a much larger area that included the installation but also included more urban and higher cost areas.

We also considered a special situation at Travis Air Force Base, where the January 2000 allowance rates declined even though the local housing market was experiencing rapid rental rate inflation—about 15 percent annually according to local officials. Rental cost data collected by Travis officials indicated that local rental costs were 12 percent higher than indicated by the contractor. This situation had led these officials to question the accuracy of the local cost data collected by DOD's contractor.

On the basis of our review, we believe that the rate problem at Travis was not caused by inaccurate contractor-collected data but rather by a combination of several factors, including the lag between the time that the contractor collected rental cost data and the effective date of the rates; the change to and full implementation of a standard-based allowance program; and DOD-imposed rules affecting final allowance rates in some areas, including Travis.

First, Travis collected rental costs 7 months after the contractor and used a weighted average technique, which the contractor did not use. Using non-weighted data, the difference between Travis' and the contractor's costs was about 9 percent—an amount consistent with the stated rate of inflation for the area. Under DOD's rate-setting process for developing allowance rates, the contractor collects rental cost data several months before the resulting rates become effective. As a result, the rates can lag behind actual rental costs in areas, such as Travis, that experience rapid rental rate inflation.

The contractor's rental cost data for Travis actually showed a 12-percent increase in local rental costs during 1999-2000. However, as part of the transition to the new allowance program, the 1999 rates were not based solely on the local cost of housing but rather on an adjustment to the 1998 rates, which were still based on housing expenditures. With full implementation of the new program in 2000, rates were based on the local cost of the housing standards for the first time. As a result, if most members in a particular pay grade had been spending more for housing than the average cost of the housing standard for their pay grade, then their rates declined.

Complicating the matter at Travis, DOD imposed rules on the final 2000 rates that resulted in Travis' rates being about 5 percent lower than indicated by the contractor's housing cost data. The rules were designed to moderate the effect of possible errors in data collection but worked to the disadvantage of areas such as Travis.

Problems in the Rate-Setting Process

Although the local housing cost data used to determine rates was accurate, DOD concluded from its review that the rate-setting process had some shortcomings. For example, DOD concluded that the process could result in rental housing units selected for rate sampling that were not appropriate for military families because the units were in poor condition or located in undesirable neighborhoods. As a result, if the rental rates for these units were lower than the average rental rate for adequate units, then the final allowance rates for the area would be inaccurately set too low.

DOD determined that some units selected for rate sampling in the Tacoma, Washington, area were not appropriate and that the 2000 housing allowance rates for the area would have been higher if only appropriate units had been included in the rental rate samples. From our own observations, some of the housing units included in the rental rate sampling for the Tacoma area either were in disrepair or were in areas that DOD officials consider inappropriate for military families. These inappropriate housing units, however, were not typical of the units included in the rental rate sampling for the Tacoma area. Almost all housing units included in the samples were considered appropriate.

- DOD identified several reasons that resulted in the inappropriate rental properties being included in rate samples:
- The process called for the contractor to identify appropriate neighborhoods for rental rate sampling by screening postal zip codes in each geographic area to identify those with average civilian income levels comparable to the average military incomes associated with each housing standard. However, screening by zip code to identify acceptable sampling areas was imprecise and failed to exclude areas containing neighborhoods with unacceptable housing.
- The process called for the contractor to use newspaper advertisements to select specific rental housing units from the identified zip codes for rate sampling. The process did not require the contractor to obtain the detailed knowledge and use the expertise of installation housing managers to help identify neighborhoods appropriate for rental rate sampling.

- The process did not require the contractor to visit installations and directly observe rental properties selected for rate sampling to help ensure that properties were appropriate for military members and their families.

DOD also concluded from its review that the process used to estimate the utility cost portion of the housing allowance could be improved. In developing the 2000 rates, DOD obtained average utility consumption data for each of the housing standards on a county-by-county basis. With this data, DOD estimated utility costs for all military installations located in each county. However, because many counties are quite large and utility consumption can vary substantially within the various areas of such counties, DOD concluded that the utility cost estimates for some installations could be inaccurate.

DOD Actions to Improve the Rate-Setting Process

Because of the shortcomings in the rate-setting process and the inconsistency between declining rates and DOD's new initiative to increase housing allowances, DOD decided in March 2000 to revert to the higher 1999 rates in all areas where rates had decreased. According to headquarters officials in each service, the reversion to the old rates reduced many of the concerns expressed by servicemembers regarding the January 2000 housing allowance rates.

- DOD also implemented several changes to improve the process that would be used to determine the 2001 rates. Specifically, DOD
- improved the precision in the contractor's income-level screening of areas for rate sampling by changing the basis used from zip codes to census tracks, which normally include much smaller areas,
- increased the participation of local installation officials in the rate-setting process by requesting each installation to identify specific neighborhoods that the contractor should use to select rental units for rate sampling,
- required the contractor to visit 50 installations during the rental rate sampling process to directly observe and photograph typical units included in the rate samples, and
- changed the methodology for estimating utility costs by using detailed climate information from the National Oceanographic Data Center as the basis for estimating utility costs.

DOD and service headquarters officials stated that the changes were successfully implemented and resulted in an accurate determination of 2001 housing allowance rates. However, under the improved process, the 2001 rates for many members should have decreased from the levels in place after the March 2000 rate reversion. DOD recognized that if the

January 2001 rates were allowed to decrease, many of the same concerns expressed about the January 2000 rate decreases would surface again— such as the fairness of two members in the same pay grade at the same location receiving different housing allowances and the inconsistency of declining rates when DOD has an initiative to increase rates.

In view of these concerns, in December 2000, before the 2001 rates became effective, the Secretary of Defense approved a new policy to provide geographic rate protection. Under this policy, DOD will not allow any rates to decrease below current levels during the time that DOD is implementing its initiative to eliminate average out-of-pocket housing costs. DOD estimated that the decision to prevent any housing allowance rates from declining in 2001 would cost about $50 million and directed the services to realign funds for 2001 to pay for the higher costs.

DOD officials also stated that they had decided to address the issue of rates lagging behind housing costs in areas experiencing rapid rental rate inflation. Local rental housing cost data will continue to be collected from May through July. In late November, before rates are finalized, DOD plans to have its contractor perform a limited telephone survey to update rental rates in those areas known to be experiencing rapidly increasing housing costs. If the survey shows that costs have increased substantially since the earlier data was collected, DOD plans to adjust the final rates.

Further, DOD officials noted that some areas of the country have recently experienced rapidly increasing utility costs. As a result, the officials stated that they plan to consider adjusting the utility cost estimates before establishing the final rates each year in January. DOD may adjust the final rates if it knows that local utility costs have increased significantly since the utility cost estimates were made from May through July, or will increase significantly in the near future.

DOD officials stated that details for implementing these new procedures should be finalized before the 2002 rates become effective.

Further Improvements Are Possible in the Rate-Setting Process

DOD responded quickly to the concerns about the January 2000 housing allowance rates and made many changes to improve the rate-setting process. However, further improvements are possible. First, questions remain concerning the appropriateness of the housing standards DOD uses to determine the rates for each military pay grade. Second, the basis for the rates established for each geographic area is not clear to many installation housing managers and servicemembers.

Concerns Over Housing Standards

Service headquarters officials stated that some members believe that the standards have not been properly associated with military pay grades. The officials noted that when DOD determined standards on the basis of housing occupied by civilians with comparable incomes, DOD did not consider as part of military income the special pay and bonuses received by many members. As a result, the rates established on the basis of the standards make appropriate housing unaffordable for members in some military pay grades. Some officials stated that the minimum standard for members with dependents in the lowest pay grades should be a two-bedroom townhouse instead of a two-bedroom apartment and that the standard for members with dependents in pay grade E-7 should be a single-family detached house instead of a townhouse.

According to DOD and service officials, differences in housing standards depending on whether a member lives on base in government housing or off base in private housing also have caused member concerns. The key difference is in out-of-pocket housing costs—members living in government housing do not pay out-of-pocket housing costs, but members living in private housing are expected to pay some out-of-pocket costs. DOD is addressing this issue through its initiative to eliminate average out-of-pocket housing costs over the next few years. However, another difference is that a member's family size is considered only when the member lives on base. For example, if living on base, a junior enlisted member in pay grade E-3 with three dependents would normally be assigned to a 3-bedroom townhouse or single-family detached house. However, if living in civilian housing off base, the housing standard used to determine the allowance rate for this member is a two-bedroom apartment. According to DOD officials, this disparity is another cause for many of the complaints concerning housing allowance rates.

DOD is studying the issues related to housing standards and allowance rates. According to DOD officials, the study will require 2 or 3 years before any recommendations for change would be proposed.

Basis for Rates Is Not Clear to Installation Housing Managers

DOD normally publishes new housing allowance rates for all areas in December, shortly before the new rates become effective on January 1. Basically, this is the only rate information available to local officials because DOD does not routinely provide installation officials with details on how the housing allowance rates for their areas are established each year. Officials at the three installations we visited—Travis Air Force Base and McChord Air Force Base and Fort Lewis in Washington—stated that the detailed basis for the rates at their installations was not clear. They stated that as a result, they lacked assurance that the rates were well-supported and calculated correctly. Further, when members raised questions about how their rates were determined, installation officials stated that they could only provide a general overview of the rate-setting process but not specific details, such as the number of rental rate samples taken, the local rental cost estimates used for each housing standard, the estimates used for utility costs and renter's insurance, and the reasons for any DOD adjustments to the data when determining the final rates.

Service headquarters officials agreed that installation housing managers need better documentation and explanation of the basis for the rates established for their installations. They stated that improved understanding of the data supporting the rates would increase local confidence in the rate-setting process.

Conclusions

DOD responded quickly to the concerns about the January 2000 housing allowance rates and took steps to address the concerns and improve the process used to determine allowance rates for 2001. However, because DOD does not routinely provide detailed feedback to installation officials explaining the basis for the rates for their areas, these officials lack confidence that the process is accurate and cannot adequately respond to members' questions about how their allowance rates were determined. Without a clear understanding of the basis for their allowance rates, servicemembers can also lose trust in the rate development process.

Recommendation

To ensure that the process for developing allowance rates is open and understandable at the installation level, we recommend that the Secretary of Defense direct the Under Secretary of Defense for Personnel and Readiness to provide housing officials at each major installation detailed information showing the basis for their established annual housing allowance rates. The information should include the number of rental rate samples taken, the average local rental cost used for each housing standard, the estimates used for utility costs and renter's insurance, and an explanation of any adjustments made to the final rates.

Agency Comments And Our Evaluation

In written comments on a draft of this report, DOD agreed with the contents of the report and concurred with the recommendation. DOD stated that installation commanders need to be provided with additional information on the results of the rate-setting process and the basis for the allowance rates. DOD stated that it currently provides the military services with details on the rates established for their installations and will encourage the services to share this data with each installation. In view of the importance of this information to installation officials, we believe that the Secretary should direct the services to provide it as we recommended rather than simply encourage them to do so.

Scope And Methodology

We performed our work at the Office of the Secretary of Defense and the headquarters of the Army, the Navy, the Air Force, and the Marine Corps. We also visited three installations that had expressed concern about the 2000 housing allowance rates for their areas—Fort Lewis and McChord Air Force Base in the Tacoma, Washington, area and Travis Air Force Base, California. At each location, we interviewed responsible agency personnel and reviewed applicable policies, procedures, and documents. We also obtained information from DOD's contractor for obtaining local housing cost information, Runzheimer International.

To determine the reasons that many January 2000 allowance rates decreased, we reviewed the history and objectives of the housing allowance program and the allowance program it replaced, examined the policies and procedures established for setting rates, reviewed the data and documentation supporting the final January 2000 rates, compared contractor-collected rental cost data with fair market rent data developed by HUD, discussed the rate development process and outcomes with DOD and service headquarters officials and with officials at the installations visited, and observed rental housing units used for rate sampling at the installations visited.

To determine DOD's response to the rate decreases, we discussed the results of DOD's review of the rate-setting process with DOD and service headquarters officials and with officials at the installations visited, documented the changes DOD made in the rate-setting process for 2001, reviewed and compared the final housing allowance rates for 2000 with 2001 rates, and discussed with DOD headquarters officials additional changes planned for the rate-setting process.

To identify any improvements DOD might make to the rate-setting process, we obtained views from DOD and service headquarters officials and officials at the installations visited concerning the effectiveness of changes already made to the rate-setting process and the need for any additional changes. We also reviewed past reports prepared by DOD's contractor that discussed possible improvements to the rate development process.

We conducted our review from August 2000 through February 2001 in accordance with generally accepted government auditing standards.

We are sending copies of this report to the Honorable Donald H. Rumsfeld, Secretary of Defense; the Honorable Joseph W. Westphal, Acting Secretary of the Army; the Honorable Robert B. Pirie, Jr., Acting Secretary of the Navy; the Honorable Lawrence J. Delaney, Acting Secretary of the Air Force; General James L. Jones, Commandant of the Marine Corps, and appropriate congressional committees. We will also make copies available to others upon request.

If you or your staff have any questions concerning this report, please call William Beusse at (202) 512-3517 or me at (202) 512-5140. Major contributors to this report were Gary Phillips and Jim Ellis.

Carol R Schuster

Carol R. Schuster
Director, Defense Capabilities
  and Management

Appendix I: Comments From the Department of Defense

OFFICE OF THE ASSISTANT SECRETARY OF DEFENSE
4000 DEFENSE PENTAGON
WASHINGTON, DC 20301-4000

FORCE MANAGEMENT
POLICY

0 2 APR 2001

Ms. Carol Schuster
Director, Defense Capabilities
   and Management
U.S. General Accounting Office
Washington, D.C. 20548

Dear Ms. Schuster:

This is the Department of Defense response to the General Accounting Office (GAO) draft report, "DOD PERSONNEL: 'Improvements Made to Housing Allowance Rate-Setting Process,' dated March 9, 2001 (GAO Code 702088/OSD Case 3053)." The Department concurs with the draft report and the recommendation. The Department's comments on the recommendation are enclosed.

If you require additional information, please contact Dr. Saul Pleeter at (703) 695-9371. The Department appreciates the opportunity to comment on the draft report. Thank you for your interest in this matter.

Sincerely,

P.A. TRACEY
Vice Admiral, USN
Deputy Assistant Secretary
(Military Personnel Policy)

Enclosure

GAO DRAFT REPORT – DATED MARCH 9, 2001
GAO CODE 702088/OSD CASE 3053

**"DOD PERSONNEL: IMPROVEMENTS MADE TO
HOUSING ALLOWANCE RATE-SETTING PROCESS"**

**DEPARTMENT OF DEFENSE COMMENTS
TO THE RECOMMENDATION**

RECOMMENDATION: To ensure that the process for developing allowance
rates is open and understandable at the installation level, the GAO recommended
that the Secretary of Defense direct the Under Secretary of Defense for Personnel
and Readiness to provide housing officials at each major installation detailed
information showing the basis for their established annual housing allowance rates.
The information should include the number of rental rate samples taken, the average
local rental cost used for each housing standard, the estimates used for utility costs
and renter's insurance, and explanation of any adjustments made to the final rates.
(p. 16/GAO Draft Report)

DOD RESPONSE: Concur. The Department agrees that the installation
commanders need to be provided with additional information as to the housing
market survey results and the basis for determination of the BAH rates. This will
not only provide them with direct feedback to their data gathering efforts but will
also make the BAH process more understandable. The Department currently
provides this information to each of the services. The Department provides a
summary report on the performance of each of the installation's housing office's
data gathering efforts. It also provides to each service a summary of the local
median housing costs for each military housing area after additional quality checks
and adjustments have been made within the Department. This summary table
includes the number of rental samples, the median local rental cost for each
standard, the utility cost and the amount for renter's insurance. The Department
would encourage each service to share this data with each installation.

Appendix II: Housing Standards and Basic Allowance for Housing Rates

As the basis for establishing servicemember basic allowance for housing rates, the Department of Defense (DOD) uses the costs of adequate housing for civilians with comparable incomes.[1] To do this, DOD has identified six housing standards, ranging from a one-bedroom apartment to a four-bedroom, single-family detached house and has applied, or anchored, a standard to each military rank, or pay grade, matching the type of housing normally occupied by civilians with comparable incomes.[2] DOD established separate housing standards for members with and without dependents and established a method to ensure that allowance rates would increase with each pay grade. Using the housing standards and the local costs of each standard in about 350 geographic areas of the country, DOD establishes the allowance rates for each year.

Tables 1 and 2 show the program's housing standards for members with and without dependents and show how rates increase with each pay grade. As an illustration, consider an enlisted member with dependents in pay grade E-7. Table 1 shows that the housing standard for this member is a three-bedroom townhouse or duplex. However, the allowance rate for this member is equal to the average local cost of a three-bedroom townhouse plus 36 percent of the difference in this cost and the average local cost of the next higher housing standard—a three-bedroom single family house. In January 2000, the national average monthly housing allowance for this member was $806, with the typical member paying $186 out-of-pocket for housing and utilities.

---

[1]See the National Defense Authorization Act for Fiscal Year 1998, Pub. L. 105-85, sec. 603.

[2]For compensation, DOD used regular military compensation for each pay grade. Regular military compensation includes basic pay, housing and subsistence allowances, and the tax advantage from the nontaxable housing and subsistence allowances.

Table 1: Allowance Program Housing Standards for Members with Dependents

Pay grade	DOD's housing standard		Allowance rate is anchor rate plus this percentage of the difference with the next higher anchor rate	January 2000 national average monthly housing allowance rate	January 2000 national average monthly out-of-pocket amount
E-1,E-2		2-bedroom apartment	0%	$564	$130
E-3	Anchor	2-bedroom apartment	0%	564	130
E-4		2-bedroom apartment	39%	603	140
E-5	Anchor	2-bedroom townhouse/duplex	0%	665	154
O-1		2-bedroom townhouse/duplex	11%	676	156
O-2		2-bedroom townhouse/duplex	98%	757	175
E-6	Anchor	3-bedroom townhouse/duplex	0%	758	176
W-1		3-bedroom townhouse/duplex	1%	759	176
E-7		3-bedroom townhouse/duplex	36%	806	186
O-1E		3-bedroom townhouse/duplex	44%	815	189
W-2		3-bedroom townhouse/duplex	52%	827	191
E-8		3-bedroom townhouse/duplex	75%	857	198
O-2E		3-bedroom townhouse/duplex	93%	879	204
O-3		3-bedroom townhouse/duplex	98%	886	205
W-3	Anchor	3-bedroom single family house	0%	888	206
E-9		3-bedroom single family house	16%	920	213
W-4		3-bedroom single family house	22%	933	216
O-3E		3-bedroom single family house	26%	940	218
W-5		3-bedroom single family house	48%	983	228
O-4		3-bedroom single family house	58%	1,005	233
O-5	Anchor	4-bedroom single family house	0%	1,088	252
O-6		4-bedroom single family house	1%a	1,097	254
O-7		4-bedroom single family house	2% a	1,109	257

Note: The National Defense Authorization Act for Fiscal Year 2001, Pub. L. 106-398, sec. 607, required a change in the housing standard used to determine allowance rates for members with dependents in pay grades E-1 through E-4. Beginning on July 1, 2001, the allowance rate for these members will be based on the average local cost of a two-bedroom apartment, plus 50 percent of the cost difference between a two-bedroom apartment and a two-bedroom townhouse.

ªFor these pay grades, the allowance rates are equal to the rate for a 4-bedroom single family house increased by the indicated percentage.

Source: DOD

Table 2: Allowance Program Housing Standards for Members Without Dependents

Pay grade	DOD's housing standard		Allowance rate is anchor rate plus this percentage of the difference with the next higher anchor rate	January 2000 national average monthly housing allowance rate	January 2000 national average monthly out-of-pocket amount
E-1,E-2		1-bedroom apartment	0%	$477	$110
E- 3		1-bedroom apartment	0%	477	110
E-4	Anchor	1-bedroom apartment	0%	477	110
E-5		1-bedroom apartment	67%	535	124
O-1	Anchor	2-bedroom apartment	0%	564	130
E-6		2-bedroom apartment	7%	570	132
W-1		2-bedroom apartment	31%	595	138
E-7		2-bedroom apartment	53%	618	143
O-2		2-bedroom apartment	83%	648	150
O-1E	Anchor	2-bedroom townhouse/duplex	0%	665	154
W-2		2-bedroom townhouse/duplex	19%	683	158
E-8		2-bedroom townhouse/duplex	20%	684	158
O-2E		2-bedroom townhouse/duplex	44%	707	163
E-9		2-bedroom townhouse/duplex	51%	713	165
W-3		2-bedroom townhouse/duplex	54%	716	165
O-3		2-bedroom townhouse/duplex	64%	725	168
O-3E	Anchor	3-bedroom townhouse/duplex	0%	759	175
W-4		3-bedroom townhouse/duplex	9%	771	178
O-4		3-bedroom townhouse/duplex	40%	811	187
W-5		3-bedroom townhouse/duplex	45%	817	189
O-5		3-bedroom townhouse/duplex	63%	842	194
O-6	Anchor	3-bedroom single family house	0%	889	205
O-7		3-bedroom single family house	2% a	907	209

ªFor this pay grade, the allowance rate is equal to the rate for a 3-bedroom single family house increased by the indicated percentage.

Source: DOD

Ordering Information

The first copy of each GAO report is free. Additional copies of reports are $2 each. A check or money order should be made out to the Superintendent of Documents. VISA and MasterCard credit cards are also accepted.

Orders for 100 or more copies to be mailed to a single address are discounted 25 percent.

Orders by mail:
U.S. General Accounting Office
P.O. Box 37050
Washington, DC 20013

Orders by visiting:
Room 1100
700 4th St., NW (corner of 4th and G Sts. NW)
Washington, DC 20013

Orders by phone:
(202) 512-6000
fax: (202) 512-6061
TDD (202) 512-2537

Each day, GAO issues a list of newly available reports and testimony. To receive facsimile copies of the daily list or any list from the past 30 days, please call (202) 512-6000 using a touchtone phone. A recorded menu will provide information on how to obtain these lists.

Orders by Internet
For information on how to access GAO reports on the Internet, send an e-mail message with "info" in the body to:

Info@www.gao.gov

or visit GAO's World Wide Web home page at:

http://www.gao.gov

To Report Fraud, Waste, and Abuse in Federal Programs

Contact one:

- Web site: http://www.gao.gov/fraudnet/fraudnet.htm
- E-mail: fraudnet@gao.gov
- 1-800-424-5454 (automated answering system)

PRINTED ON RECYCLED PAPER

CPSIA information can be obtained at www.ICGtesting.com
Printed in the USA
BVOW03s1221110615

404240BV00011B/114/P